T0328482

these hands

Makhosazana Xaba

these hands

Makhosazana Xaba

modjaji books

This edition published in 2017 by Modjaji Books.

The first edition of *these hands* was published in 2005
by Timbila Poetry Project

ISBN: 978-1-928215-27-1

Cover Artwork: Nala Xaba
Typesetting and design: Louise Topping

www.modjajibooks.co.za

Contents

For Nala

It has been a joy to walk next to you on your journey

It has been a wonder to watch your creativity unfold

Uze ungakhohlwa ukuthi ngohlala ngikuthanda

X-Himself and Song

Looking in his face, you would think he was the composer.
Watching his body move, you would think he created movement.
His fingers, in motion, got you, instantly, in motion.
He ensouled you with his voice,
his thick, malleable lips, his every bit of body.

Wasuphuka, wasiphuka, wasiphuka,
wasiphuka wenyuka
Wenyuka, wenyuka uApollo
Apollo Eleven! Every child got to know
in the back of beyond - Ndaleni, where I grew up.
The composer put the words in song
My father made it come alive
without the TV images
We had our own visual artist.
We saw Apollo Eleven shoot out
into the galaxy, through his every bit of body.

To the Durban July, I still haven't been
I have zero knowledge of horse racing
But, through his every bit of body, I love horses
Because when he sang:
Uponi ihashi lami engilithandayo
Uponi ihashi lami engilithandayo
Uponi ihashi lami engilithandayo
Ihash' engilithandayo
Uponi ihashi lami engilithandayo
Ihashi lami engilithandayo,

you had no choice but to fall in love with horses
You started believing that he created horses.

My father must have lived in the souls of many composers.
A conductor of note, with a voice you would give your vote.

9

An educator extra-ordinaire
because his choice of loved songs must have been
for nurturing the young.
Why else did he love the great King Kong song
on the politics of poverty?
With that song
I didn't need social scientists,
I didn't need political scientists to give me loads of notes
on apartheid's greatest crimes or capitalism's gravest sins.
Through his every bit of body
I knew that, I heard it, I lived it:
Hambani madoda, niyemsebenzini
Vukani bafazi siyahlupheka
Amakhaza nemvula
Ibhasi igcwele
Sihlushwa
Otsotsi besikhuthuza
Siyaphela indlala
Nemali Ayikho
Hambani madoda
Isikhathi isikho

Through his every bit of body
even Christianity took an unexpected turn
because he knew the great composers who
had the skill to transform
what was alien and alienating
into something familiar, to be embraced.
When Jesus Christ is all of a sudden
born in Qhudeni, near Nquthu, you can't but sit up and listen.
Then you touch the blue African skies
on his every bit of body. You hear the lowveld's serenity,
then you smell the water from the stream
and the dead night comes alive.

From the peaceful valleys of Qhudeni
a true Christmas carol for Africa
He made it worth knowing,
he made it worth singing, through his every bit of body:
Kuzolile ebusuku
Eduze naseQhudeni
Abelusi bezinkomo
Bangazelele lutho
Kwavela ukukhanya okukhulu
Besaba bawela phansi
Bathuthumela

Well, I too, like the shepherds,
I do thuthumela at the thought that to this day
I still have not been to his grave
because all this time
I have not been able to forget the pain,
the sorrow, the misery, he brought to the family
with his love of the bottle.

He sang these songs at night
in the mornings
in the small hours of the mornings,
sometimes with his friends
oftentimes alone
sometimes with his tuning fork in his right hand
oftentimes on his feet
other times on his behind
sometimes on their bed next to my mom
oftentimes with us watching.
And, at times, demanding we sang along.

I watched my mother lose her smile,
her laughter, her humour, because of him.

I watched my big brother lose inner peace, because of him.
I watched myself lose hope, clutching despair, because of him
His love of the bottle went through his every bit of body,
destroying what love I could have had for him.

He died on Monday morning, 13 April 1998
in his sleep, in his bed, at home.
His liver fed up, his heart gave up.

That morning, at my Johannesburg home,
I sang one of the songs about death that he so loved:
Ngimbeleni phansi kontshani duze nezihlahla zomnyezane
Ngimbeleni phansi kotshani
Duze nazo ezomnyezane
Ngozwa nami lapho ngilele utshani ngaphezulu buhleba
Utshani ngaphezulu buhleba

I do not know what type of grass is growing on his grave.
I do know we did not bury him next to the willow trees.
I do trust that he continues to hear the grass whisper, as he wished.

What I do know is that his music lives in me
His voice will forever pierce through me
as it always pierced through his every bit of body.

Through his every bit of body,
his tuning fork in his right hand,
his tapping feet, his thick, malleable lips,
I feel the staff notation,
I smell *do-re-mi-fa-so-la-ti-do*,
I hear the *crescendo*,
I touch forte, *fortissimo*,
I taste p, pp, *pianissimo*.

The war America wants

"Ma, there's something I don't understand."
I give her a quick glance
while minding the wheel,
watching rush hour traffic.
Hmm..., I say, in a manner that says:
I'm listening.

"How can America and Iraq be at war?"
I see the frown,
quizzical, familiar.
Hmm..., I say, in a manner that says:
I'm interested.

"Because when American soldiers
get into the plane to go to Iraq,
the soldiers in Iraq
get into the plane to go to America
so they each have no one to fight with."

I smile,
she is ten.
I frown,
hoping wisdom reaches my lips.

Then, in typical Nala style,
hands in the air, she concludes:
"I think Americans are stupid.
They are the ones that want this war,
hey, Mama?"
 I turn, give her a quick glance.
My silent look,
our mother–daughter lingo,
tells her how I feel.

I watch rush hour traffic,
mind the wheel
on our way home.

Whirlwind

Sucked in by the swirling whirlwind,
turning around its epicenter,
twirling swiftly,
I can do nothing but watch you,
wait for you to emerge
out of the riot.
I can do nothing but hope that,
when the whirlwind subsides
and you surface,
you'll not only be whole,
but you'll be facing in the right direction,
the direction, right for you.

The language of knowing

I learnt a new language recently
without the aid of a tutor
without meaning to.
I learnt it without the aid of a book
a language laboratory
an immersion course
a mother-tongue speaker
or even a compact disk.
It's a universal language
a common language
I have now come to know.

It's the language of looking
of looking and seeing
seeing then knowing
knowing without evidence
beyond the looking.

No one warned me about this language
without words, sentences or grammar
codes, signs or gestures
dialects or accents.

This magical language of looking
connecting through the eyes
shared with complete strangers.
The language of recognising community
through seeing and knowing.

These hands

These hands know putrid pus from oozing wounds.
They know the musty feel of varying forms of faecal formations.

They know the warmth of gushing blood from gaping bodily spaces.
They know of mucous, sliding out of varying orifices.

These hands remember the metallic feel of numerous guns,
when the telling click was heard.
They recall the rumbling palm embrace over grenades
ready for the release of mortal destruction.

These hands will never forget the prickling touch of barbed wire on border
fences.
These hands can still feel the roughness of unknown tree leaves
that served as toilet paper in bushes far away.

These hands have felt pulsating hearts over extended abdomens
They know the depth of vaginas, the opening mouths of wombs
They know the grasp of minute, minute-old clenched fists.

These hands have squeezed life's juice from painful pounding breasts.
These hands have made love, producing vibrations from receiving lovers.

These hands have pressed buttons, knobs and switches
They have turned screws and wound clocks
Steered wheels and dug holes
Held instruments, implements and ligaments
Moulded monuments, created crafts, healed hearts.

These hands now caress the keyboard
fondle pens that massage papers
weaning fear, weaving words
wishing with every fingerprint
that this relationship will last forever.

Malume

In his message, "Fare thee well, Comrade Zinjiva"
Raks called you a soldier-poet of note.
To me, you were Malume
the malume who told me stories
about the early days of the ANC
stories of the heated debates within the ANC
stories of umkatashinga within Mkhonto weSizwe.
To me you were Malume, the storyteller
the malume I never had at home.

Raks called you a diplomat par excellence.
To me, you were Malume.
You told me stories about foreign countries
The breathing, talking, laughing pictures
of lives in those countries now hang in my mind's eyes
your voice, an ornamental frame around each one.

Raks called you father-husband, all rolled in one.
To me, you were Malume.
We cooked and ate together
We made rules about how to use the toilet
when to flush and when to not
as water rations and nocturnal noise were an issue.

You were the malume we waited for on those nights
when a serious story hit the news
because we knew when you came home
there would be more stories to listen to;
For any news item of the day
could turn into a long history lesson in the evening.
Malume, weaver of words
we sat in your bedroom many a night
catching droplets of wisdom from your lips.

Raks called you an activist, a philosopher.
To me, you were a malume
who came home drunk on some days
asked us to hide your other bottles
until you are sober and ready to partake again.
We sat at our kitchen bench many a day
discussing our meagre finances
which mphando item to sell next
so we could afford another meal.

I heard via Raks' e-mail of your death
a month and more after your burial.
How can a diplomat par excellence die
without this even becoming news?
In frustration I asked around
only to confirm your passing had not hit the hot news list.
I thought back to the months when I last visited
you at your Judith's Paarl home.
I thought back to the Lusaka that is now our history.
I awoke to the fact that I carry into the future
the verbal tapestry you crafted.
I carry your voice into tomorrow.
I carry a malume who spiced my life.

To me, you were neither a comrade nor Bra Vic.
Neither Victor Matlou nor Zinjiva Nkondo.
Thank you for being my family too.

Heart surgery

"Good morning,
thank you for calling Voyager.
My name is Thuli.
How can I be of assistance?"

Oh, good morning.
I need to check if
I have enough miles
to fly from Johannesburg to Cape Town,
round trip, as soon as possible.

"Voyager number, please, madam?"
Oh I have it right here: 12 15 22 5.
"12 15 22 5?"
Yes, that's right.

"Can you hold one sec for me, madam?
Madam I'm afraid
you don't have ..."
No! No! I have an emergency.
I have to get to Groote Schuur Hospital
I have this heart problem - my heart moved!
"Pardon me?"
I said my heart moved!
It's beating in the wrong places.
"Madam, I don't understand?"
I need a heart surgeon.
I need one now!
My heart thunders in my neck,
it pulsates in my abdomen,
beats in my inner thighs
and sends rushes of blood everywhere!

"I beg you pardon, madam?"
Since I sat my eyes on her
my heart has gone haywire!
"Excuse me, madam, I really think
you have the wrong number."

Oh, I'm sorry.
Did you say
I don't have enough miles
on my account?
"Uh, uh, yes, madam.
Let me see.
Would you like to hold on?
Just one sec ..."

Weaving silk

My bed is not made yet
so, I will not curl up and sleep.
The sheets are crumpled
the duvet is a heap of fabric
the pillows sprawl, looking lost.
Even the mattress is skew on its base.

I love the touch of fresh clean sheets.
They have to be warm to the skin, soft as silk.
I will weave the silk myself, if I have to.

Although my eyes want to close
my limbs go limp under my frame
my heart beats with a retiring pace
my bed has to be made
just the way I like it
before I go to sleep.

The silence of a lifetime

At seven she was raped
by her uncle
in the middle of the night
under a dining table
in the lounge-cum-dining room
of their four-roomed home
in the township
where 11 of them lived.

Everyone else was asleep
on every available floor space.
She muffled her cries
as his penis suffocated her.
He kept whispering to her:
"Don't ever tell anyone".

At 15 she was gang-raped
by four classmates
in broad day light
on a desk
in their classroom
at their school
where just under a thousand of them studied.
Everyone else was in their little corner
on the grounds of the school premises.
She cried out loud.
As each boy muffled her cries with a punch.
Numbed with pain, she kept hearing them:
"Stop thinking you're so smart".

At 18 she was date-raped
by her first boyfriend
just before ten at night
on a concrete pavement

behind the movie theatre
in a city
where millions of city dwellers breathe and stroll.
Everyone else was on their own important mission
on the streets, in the corners of the city.
She cried silently
as she wondered madly
what had suddenly gone wrong
with her very first boyfriend,
as he kept saying:
"Prove that you love me".

At 26 she was raped in marriage
by her husband
at six o'clock in the morning
on their matrimonial bed
while their child was feeding on her breast
in their home
where no one would question why.
Everyone else was minding their business,
whatever it is at this time of the day.
She swallowed to muffle the anger
as her baby swallowed the breast milk.
She heard him say, at one point:
"You are my wife, aren't you?"

At 45 she was raped
by two of her colleagues
on a sunny weekend afternoon
in her own flat,
in her own lounge,
where anyone who walked in there
did so at her invitation.
The work had been done,

the report written,
when her colleagues took her by surprise.
Everyone else was minding their own business
as they do every weekend afternoon.
Her cries went nowhere.
Her colleagues had turned the music system on full blast.
As they took turns, they each muttered:
"So, who's the boss now?
This boardroom is much better
than the one at work, hey, Sweetie?"

At 60 she was raped
by the neighbour she knew so well
one wet Sunday morning
on the path from church,
amongst the mielie fields
where everyone walked by
every single day of the year
in this small community,
in this tiny village
where the villagers lived in peaceful harmony.
Every villager was minding their own business,
whatever it is they did on a rainy Sunday morning.
She could not even cry
for the shock of what was happening was numbing.
She kept telling herself she was dreaming
though she knew she was hearing right
when he kept saying:
"When last did you get it, old woman?
Enjoy it. No one else wants an old rag like you."

Words

Whenever I take the pulse
of my existence
feel the pinch
of my persistence
against the grinding grain
of my resistance
to the pounding punch
of their insistence,
words transmit to me
a drumroll of deliverance.

The brown pelican

It took the harbour walk, four days later
to stop wishing you were here.
Watching the hunting pelican,
near and distant boats' lights all around
flickering in the dark waters
of an early Key West night.

Standing, taking in the moist warm air
I watched the big brown bird below
the belly of its military beak ballooning,
sideways and downwards,
looming loose, pale pink,
catching dinner, seemingly impatiently.
I wondered; was it getting enough?

Then, suddenly, you were there.
I smelt you, felt your breasts against my back
your broad right arm over my right shoulder
your playful fingers on my collar bone.
I wondered where your left arm was
wondered what expression was on your face?

The pelican, with hungry eyes,
guarding a beak as long as my forearm
was determined to go to bed on a full stomach.
I wondered; are you wet?
The pelican was and also the minute, dark-grey fish
restlessly wiggling in the nest
of the meeting place of its mighty wings.

I wondered how long will the fish's luck last?
My luck stayed with me
as I sauntered up Simonton Street
back to my room at Pearlsrainbow,
the solemn night embracing my gait.
I savoured the moments
and thanked the brown pelican
for delivering you to me.

Your eyes

Your eyes shoot across my chest
from the crowds of colleagues in the hall
as you look up at me at the mic
the rest of panel seated behind me.

They linger with tears
in the sweltering musty hotel room
as you speak with them
into the dawning of the next day.

They screw themselves
like an electric drill slowly into mine
as we sway belly to belly on the dance floor
I look up at you, close
You are firm, warm, unfathomable.

Your eyes pierce through mine in shock
as we sit face to face
across the restaurant table and
I tell you that you make me wet.

I watch them nailed on my torso
in a crowded pillared restaurant
as I guide the group to picture
a vision far beyond the present.

I feel them vacuum my temple
from your side of the table
in the small meeting room.

I see them smile, then marvel,
then clasp themselves
onto my clothing like a dressmaker's safety pins
as I attempt to reach consensus
with a mini crowd from varying African hills.
With them you brush my tears aside as we say goodbye.

Your eyes have been gliding
over the moons of time for over a year now
greeting mine, meeting mine, breeding.
Now they are plastered between the sclera
and retina of both of my eyes
But, I still don't know what colour they are.

Silent sibling summit

What shall we tell the children?
How exactly shall we say it to our children?
That one of them, one of us, our blood
held a gun at a stranger
to get a lift back home,
threw the driver in the veld
to get a car radio to sell.

Once, a gun was held to my head.
Our children, I thought, should never know.
After the second time
I heard myself say, each time the story got told:
"I wish my ten-year-old daughter was not with me
when it happened."

Now this very daughter I must inform
that her own cousin,
her mother's sister's son,
her blood,
the 16-year-old she's known all her life,
on whose lap she often sat,
in whose warm, brotherly embrace she often cuddled,
on whose side she sat watching TV,
with whom she shared countless meals:
Held a gun at another. Hijacked a car.

Just how do we tell our children this?

Love poem for my writing group

It's the uncontrollable laughter that
leaves my muscles sore, exhausted
all our faces beaming at the reading.

It's the sudden silence that descends
into our bodies
permeating our beings
as the words meander through each writer-reader.
The silence settles upon us, simmers.
summoning us to sadness
as we salute our oneness.

It's breaking down barriers
the bitter barricades
begrudging our
bellowing freedom.

Solitary cloud

The desert you created
on Friday 13 July
left the soil cracking, itching, aching.
Now, a year later, the gaping crevices
hunger for raindrops to nourish, heal,
fill the gaps, soothe the pain.

Does the air smell different lately,
moist and tender, though clouds have not gathered?
Deadened, I yearn for raindrops to fall
for a river to swallow my cracked body.
I want to flow through myriad landscapes
into the roaring waters of the sea.
Once I get there waves will lift me,
carry me across the ocean to your shore.

Come and fetch me with two flasks
one with coffee, the other butternut soup.
Your car is warm, I know
but a pair of gloves, warm and ready
will help my hands thaw faster.

Woman, desert maker,
have you just moulded that solitary cloud in the sky?

Shit street

Why do I feel so much pain
in my body, as if seated
in the centre of the marrow
of every single bone?

Tears heat up in my eyes,
my heart beats faster -
any doctor will tell you it's not normal.
I sweat instantly, like a dog,
unlike I do when I jog.

Like a trained soldier I know
where to look,
how to look,
when to look.

So why do I smell shit
when I walk in the streets?
When I cannot smell the pots
burn in my kitchen?

In case you're thinking of visiting The Apartheid Museum

In case you want to go to The Apartheid Museum
take the M1 South highway, then the Xavier off-ramp,
which follows after the Booysens off-ramp.
If you are somewhere next to Gold Reef City, you should find it.

And the game plays on

When white boys played rugby
in Limpopo Province
they made a mistake,
a young a Black boy
was mistaken for a rugby ball.

When white boys played rugby
in Limpopo Province
they didn't handle
the young Black boy with care
as they do with the rugby ball.
They punched, kicked
and threw him in a dam
where he was discovered,
days later, decomposed.

The white rugby-playing boys
of Limpopo Province
are pleading "Not guilty".

When the Black masses
of Limpopo Province
cry "Foul!"
and the rest of the country's masses,
who understand only too well
the kind of rugby
that the white boys played
in Limpopo Province,
also cry "Foul"
the world watches
the new South Africa.

The world watches
from the stadiums of the universe

The world watches
as the game plays on.

Suggestions please

At the National School of the Arts the other day
What? What did you just say?
I was reminded of a question
that the Johannesburg Metropolitan Council
and nine years of democracy,
Excuse me, I didn't hear what you said?
colluding, lulled me into believing
Jou ma se gat.
I'll never hear again
Msunu kanyoko, ungijwayela kabi.

Do you work here?
(No Missus, Yes Missus,
I need a job, I'll do anything.)
My entire body transformed.
Oh, hi, my name is Khosi.
What's yours?
You are talking to me, right?
My eyes fixed on her wrinkles, her grimace.
Are you blind? I'd be in uniform if I did!

I recognised the nearly-forgotten, uniform expression
on such white women's faces.
Really, do I look like your maid?
My mind rushed back into the void of primeval files
Fuck you! Did you hear me,
I said, f...u...c...k you!
as, with disappointment, I recalled
that in all those years
Listen, I know all blacks are the same to you.
But, no, I don't work here.
I never found the perfect answer
to this perennial question.

(No, Madam, I wish I did,
I am currently unemployed.)

The void deepened
Mfazindini, uzonya ungizwa kahle.
as our eyes locked like packs of dynamite.
Masimb' akho.

I really need suggestions
Up your fat pink arse.
'cause I've clearly failed
to find a fitting response.

What, what did you just say?
Nine years! Nine years of ... WHAT?

A question of time

I see you squirm,
kick and run.
I hear you whisper,
shout and scream.

I watch you fold neatly into a ball
and roll away
only to hit against rocks
that roll you back
with the same force and speed.

So I know now
that you know
that we both know
it's only a question of time.

It's a question of time before
you slow down
and walk this way
before you start
whispering in my direction
our direction, as it was meant to be.

Brakpan 2002

They knew not her name,
they knew not from whence she came.
She worked for them
in their very home.

A domestic worker,
sleeping in the backyard,
the familiar servants' quarters.

When she dared walk in the garden
two pit bulls ripped her apart,
sent her to her death.

A member of the public
killed the two dogs out of rage.
The dog owners,
home owners, white, employers,
knew not her name,
from whence she came
who worked for four months in their home.

She was just a
domestic worker, black,
in a backyard in Brakpan.
Now she lies in a mortuary.
Her dog bite-riddled body can't be claimed.
Her employers assert unashamedly that
the dogs bit her because, they too, did not know her,
because she had never walked in the garden.
She was merely a body,
a black body,
in a backyard in Brakpan
in the year 2002.

You told me

You told me you speak French,
took lessons evening after evening.
It was important to you that,
when you go on your dream holiday in Paris,
you can communicate
because the French are hostile
when you do not speak their language.

You told me you speak Yiddish
'cause your grandparents spoke it to you,
you learnt it as a child and, surprisingly,
you still speak it well, decades later.

You told me you've had
Black friends since 1976
since the struggle days
because you were involved
in the struggle for that long.
You drove comrades to their homes
after meetings, at night,
braving the drive back to your own suburb.
You met your comrades' parents, their families.
You even baby sat their children.

You told me that
you loved your nanny with all your heart
because she raised you like her own.
In fact, you told me
you used to run to her
in her servants' quarters, at the back,
when your big house in front felt lonely
and your parents were having a fight.

Yes, you even said,
you said you preferred her company
to that of your parents,
and your parents' friends,
because she sang songs to you,
put you on her lap
and rocked you to sleep
while your family
had arguments around the dinner table.

You have academic degrees,
articles published in peer-reviewed international journals.
You are a true South African who
dedicated your life to the struggle.
You told me you even had Black lovers
because colour never meant anything to you.

You also told me you have taken
so many "Zulu lessons" you have lost count.
But, because the lessons were too didactic,
the language too tonal, time too tight,
struggle meetings took too much time,
you *still* cannot speak isiZulu, or any indigenous language.

Soul-mating

Did you erect a tent inside your solar plexus?
Or was it a mud house, with a grass roof?
Did your sisters help you
mud ball by mud ball
grass stalk by grass stalk?
Or, was it a brick house, with an asbestos roof?
What did you mean when you said I've captured your soul?

I only put down the foundation,
rock upon hard, solid rock.
Now it's drying, awaiting your arrival
so we can build the walls together,
stagger over the roof in unison,
sealing it to my solar plexus so you never have to leave,
knowing the house, infused with my being,
is your choice, your labour.

Worm music

I want to dance the tango
'cause my feet are so numb.
I want to dance the tango
'cause my thighs need to thaw,
my neck needs loosening,
my eyes need to see when they look,
my waist needs to know not to waste its twist.

Then, my arms will have no choice but to reach out,
my fingers will know to grasp
and, together,
we can dance
to the rhythm of centipedes.

Waking up

In the early morning of my life
I did not hear the cocks crowing
I did not wake up as with my peers.

In the mid morning of my life
I watched the shadows move
Without much thought, I followed.

In the midday of my life
I felt the scorching heat of the sun
burn through my hair, right into my brain
I knew then that I wouldn't let the sun burn me
ever again.
I didn't go in the sun at midday again.

In the afternoon of my life
as I watch the sun set,
you rise ever so slowly behind its rays
to be my sun in the night
lighting my consciousness as I sleep
I dream, dream, dream you.
Slowly, I wake up to
you being in my life,
turning it around
moulding, it in ways I never imagined.

You, the first woman I love
in the afternoon of my life.

So

Are we about to
hear the rainbow whisper to us in seven languages
touch and hold the mirage with our four hands
taste enchanting music, with our tongues entwined?

Are we about to obliterate speech
smell each other's thoughts
inhale and exhale each other's words?

Are we indeed about to swim free style
across the botanical gardens
fighting bees for nectar, butterflies for pollen
unplugging thorns, repelling insects?

Are we just about to lay down on our backs
flesh to flesh, side by side
under a zillion orchids,
watching each petal float, lightly, slowly, downward
landing on us
till our bodies are fully covered
layered with a velvety smell
till the colour of our skins merge
radiating as one?

Sad whale-speak at Misty Cliffs

The whales here speak to people.
Last night when I got lost they told me to
ask that woman and her son where this house is.
They tell me to get up in the morning, to watch them dance.
They even remind me to cook and eat.
They warn me when the sun is about to set
so I won't miss the mesmerising splendour,
the big, hot, red ball disappearing
in the greenish-blue Atlantic waters.

There are two highly eloquent ones, a mother and her child.
They are always close by, talking to me.
Sometimes they sing,
but all the time the songs are sad.
I'm not sure why they choose sad songs to sing to me.
Maybe, in empathy, they want me to know that
coming here to be alone, to think,
was not just a good idea, it was perfect timing
because when a soul has to mourn a loss
being alone is always best.

So, then you called last night
in the tone I've come to know so well –
hurried, efficient, almost unlistening,
galloping to end the conversation.

I understand now.
The whales were preparing me
for the sad ending of something that never really was.
Something, at best,
an almost event.

Tear essence

Today, having lunch on my own
at a restaurant in Rosebank,
I pull the chair from across closer,
straighten my legs and
lay my feet on it.
I feel the absence of your thighs
on the sides of my feet,
the absence of your gentle hand
cruising my legs.
Whenever we do that
you shoot your special, familiar smile into my eyes.

Today I hear the thundering silence
of two weeks' zero communication.
The break's stone muteness hits home.
My meal is flavoured
with delicate fresh tears.

Stormy weather

Had I turned on the radio,
stayed till the end of the TV news bulletin,
I would have been warned about the storm.
Had I even peeped through my window
and freed my ears of deafening wax
instead of blissfully dreaming
I would have seen the dark clouds gathering,
the horizon darkening.
I would have known not to step out of the door
just as the jacaranda tree outside my home was giving up.
I wouldn't be buried underneath it right now,
feeling excruciating pain with the lightest move,
knowing there will be no one here to look under the fallen tree
as the heavens thunder on,
incessant, heavy raindrops reaching me through the leaves,
crackling lightning searing my eyes
underneath the fallen tree.

The only hope I've left
is knowing that storms, heavy storms,
are nature's gift.
For now, I can only lie here,
waiting for the last moment,
comforted by the age-old wisdom:
I'm a victim of nature,
just like the jacaranda tree.

A t-shirt for all seasons

Oh, ye Christians of the world,
when you are
done preaching
while your congregations
are home for
their gluttonous Sunday lunches,
visit stores where they sell t-shirts
with the inscription:
"When God created me, he just wanted to show off".

Buy them and donate them to the children.
Or, better still, use the collection
from your congregation
to set up a printing plant
for t-shirts
so you can produce these
yourselves
during the six days
when you aren't preaching sermons
that plunge our children
into confusion,
barring them from dreaming.

Jacaranda lyrics

I wanted to write a lyric
about jacaranda trees in spring,
but the council debated
about cutting them down
because they are greedy,
because they're not indigenous.

Today, getting home from work,
I found two in my neighbourhood,
corner Bezuidenhout and St Georges Road,
cut down.
Well, not completely cut down, cut back.
But what's a jacaranda tree
without its spring blossoms?

The words of the song evaporated.
It's title disappeared.
Instead of a lyric
I'll write a letter to council
to protest the absence of Jacaranda blossoms in spring.

While I wait

Are you afraid to let me into your heart,
through your arteries and veins,
for I might clog them up,
causing a stroke?

I wouldn't mind choosing your lymph glands, rather,
but, if you fear I may cause them to swell,
making your legs heavy with elephantiasis,
then I understand.

Are you afraid if I enter your lungs
I may narrow your bronchioles
leaving you without air?

Maybe I'll get a transit visa, go through your kidneys
so I can at least pass through you,
still leaving you free
to make up your mind.

I'll wait,
a thin, invisible layer on your skin,
so you can simply carry me around with you,
on you,
every second of your quivering existence.

Dignity spills

There is a war going on, South Africa.
Declare a state of emergency.

The war is undeclared.
So, the other side is caught off guard, unarmed.

The war of sons on daughters,
brothers on sisters,
uncles on aunts,
fathers on mothers,
grandfathers on grandmothers

It's a war of men on women,
of boys on girls.

The war is undeclared,
so statistics cannot be collected properly.
The war is denied by its perpetrators.
Its soldiers do not wear uniforms.
They parade in camouflage -
as loving grandfathers, fathers, uncles, brothers and sons.

Grandmothers, mothers, aunts, sisters and daughters
are caught in the intricate web of the camouflage.
The camouflage of trust,
of belief in the goodness of human nature.
The camouflage of love.

Only to be reminded
that our grandfathers, fathers, uncles, brothers and sons
are none other than soldiers of war
with hatred in their hearts,
planning to pounce at any moment
to attack, destroy, maim and kill

The commanders behave like agents.
They wear different masks,
saying one thing in public,
joining the soldiers in secret.

The war zone is not demarcated
so, the victims do not know where not to go.
The war is everywhere -
in private and public spaces,
in individual and communal places,
in sacred and unholy spaces,
in clean and dirty places.
It goes on relentlessly, unabated.

Like blood, dignity spills.
Unlike blood, dignity is unmeasured.
Wounds gape,
limbs break,
souls split.
As the war is undeclared,
the zone is not demarcated.
the anti-war volunteers - too few - know not where to go.

The latest victims: infants, children.
The "ordinary" victims: girls, women.
Even the elderly, our pensioners, do not escape.
Rape rips lives apart.
Incest rips lives apart.
Violence rips lives apart.

The war is on, South Africa.
Declare a state of emergency.
The war zone is you.

Flowering rot

I threw away
the flowers you gave me.
I threw them
into the rubbish bin
because it's Monday.
They are better out there,
with the neighbourhood's
rot and stench.

In my lounge
they were beginning
to cause me trouble,
creating emptiness,
a deep sadness in my core.
Now I am without
one more reminder
that you invaded my soul
without any warning.

(Oh, and by the way,
can't you tell
the difference between
roses and carnations?)

Handle with care

If tomorrow I awaken
in smithereens
like a glass bowl
after an explosion
on a hot stove plate
will you pick me up,
piece by piece,
moving the furniture
inch by inch?

Will you tactfully
go through the cutlery drawer
if the blast found it ajar,
uncover me amidst the clutter,
then, dress the drawer anew?

Will you look
to the far most point
from the stove
till you find
that one bit of me?

Will you shine a torch
into dark corners,
behind and around?

Will you peep through
and reach out
into lean corridors,
alongside immovables?

Will you pace gently
and if, perchance,
you step on me,

remove me?
But, taking time and care
as you would
with a farewell kiss?

Will you pour your eyes into the sink,
using the tips of your fingers
to save particles of me
from drowning
or going down the drain?

Will you flip the kitchen cloth
with tenderness so that
those bits of me
are not insulted?

Will you take a careful look
on every surface
of the kitchen cabinets
for some of me
in case I'll be resting there?

Will you venture into
the airy spaces of the kitchen
with a damp cloth
and mop the dust
in between and around
so that all of me
can be in one
as you pack me away
from your life,
in the marked space
of the graveyard
of relationships.

Acknowledgements

I would like to thank the people behind the idea of this second edition: Sisi Vuyiswa Maqagi, Jenny Bozena Du Preez and Mary West from Nelson Mandela Metropolitan University (NMMU) in Port Elizabeth. Without your interest, encouragement and concrete suggestion, this book would not have had this second life. Enkosi kakhulu! Ndiyabulela.

Eternal gratitude goes to Vonani Bila who approached me in 2002 with the idea of publishing the first edition.

Thanks to Colleen Higgs who continues to live up to the motto of Modjaji Books.

Ukuzala ukuzelula amathambo, thank you Nala, for the artwork on the cover, the book now has a new and inspiring look. And, for your incisive editing eye Nala, ngibonge kakhulu.

Thanks to Louise Topping for the beautiful design of my book.

Also by Makhosazana Xaba

Poetry
these hands
Tongues of their Mothers

Short Stories
Running & other stories

Edited Anthologies
Queer Africa: New and Collected Fiction (co-Editor)
Proudly Malawian: Life Stories from Lesbian and Gender-nonconforming Individuals (co-Editor)
Like the untouchable wind: An anthology of poems
Queer Africa 2: New Fiction (co-Editor)

Pamphlets
Start a writing group and make it work – Pamphlet 2

For Children
MaDriver is late
Imindeni
Linjani izulu?
Izinambuzane